Author: Daniel James Kellenbeck
ISBN # 978-0-692-85889-9
Copyright: 2017
Part 2 Originally Copyrighted 2003

The following work is actually two books combined under one cover.
This work is my response to terrorism.
I believe this to be a work of virtue.
I have preserved the titles of both books for they are explanatory.
My method of titling my works was inspired by the show Aesop's Fables.
My works is a testimony unto God the Father, Jesus the Christ, And the Holy Ghost.
I am a member of The Church of Jesus Christ of Latter Day Saints.
I hope however that all the world will receive my testimony for the message of Jesus is unto all mankind.

[2]

Preface

I am a man of visions but I have bipolar disorder which could be one explanation for my visionary episodes. I however believe that God has found me worthy to receive the visions of eternity. And I am also on meds for my bipolar condition. I also have found the veil throughout my life to be very transparent as I remember my experiences throughout eternity.

I believe that Jesus Christ did give me a new heart and this came from his baptism of fire I believe I received many years ago. And there came upon me many spirits of fire, and after they tested me unto perfection, one did remain behind to give my condition solution. And so I became two that have become one. And this combination did cause that I should come to put the darkness to sleep and quite frankly it had grown beyond that which I could contain. So it was that an unclean spirit or more specifically a devil was harvested from me as we two did separate.

In this body of work I tell a lot of things I remember from the being I was and also many of my visions from the being I am Become. If there be mistakes in this work they belong to me and I apologize for them. For I do not desire to give anyone bad guidance. I desire in this work to share my memories, my visions and my spirituality. If you have a good working knowledge of the scriptures you will have a better understanding of the message I seek to impart. If you have the companionship of the Holy Ghost he can bear witness to you of the things that are right for you to receive from this my work.

I am a member of the Church of Jesus Christ of Latter Day Saints and believe it to offer unto the world the saving ordinances of the gospel of Jesus Christ. I however believe that God gives to men and women that believe in the name of Jesus Christ the power to become sons and daughters of God. This is a process that can and does take time and effort, and the spirits of the adversary which includes the sons of perdition do present obstacles to this process.

I have received a baptism of proper priesthood authority unto the remission of my sins and a baptism of fire that is given of Jesus Christ. The Holy Ghost has been a strong influence in guiding my life since I Embraced the gospel. However prior to receiving the gospel mine was a life of disbelief and sins. I do not deny the darkness of my soul but Jesus came to save sinners and my mental condition does cause me to have a difficulty with the dark side and its associated violence. I would repeat I take meds also to help me with this.

In the church I believe in, we have what we call a patriarchal blessing. This is an inspired blessing you can receive, which is an opportunity for God to give an individual guidance. In my blessing it declares that I have been given the gift of interpretation. And I believe I possess a great understanding of latter day prophecy as contained in the scriptures. Also in my patriarchal blessing it states that I was "spared to live and triumph in accomplishing a great mission." We will get into the meaning of that in greater detail in the work to follow.

In the early part of this work I will tell about events which actually happened to me in my mortal life. As we progress this work will become more visionary. I would tell you that I have come to realize that receiving the visions of eternity is also a Learning process and that the visions are not absolutes. Please keep this in mind as you receive my work.

I now present you the work that I have titled "The Book of My Life" or "The Visions of Eternity."

Table of Contents

[8]

Chapter 1

When I was sixteen I died, and my spirit was brought unto God the Father and Jesus Christ to be judged. And they had a conversation with me, and between them, and I was in a difficult situation because my life had been full of sin. The Father was full of wrath towards me, but the Son did have compassion on me, mostly due to the hardships I had experienced in life, and because that is his nature. And the Son did persuade the Father to send me back into my mortality and this world. He did further declare that he wanted me to obtain joy and accomplish the mission he had called me to in the pre-existence.

I do not remember what God looked like but I do remember what euphoria I felt being in the presence of God. The Father declared that I was basking in the glories they had attained to and that I should go forth and obtain glory of my own. Now should I obtain glory for any of my actions I declare be the glory unto God. I do know however that regaining his presence is something we should desire.

I am sixty years old at the writing of this book and I have found joy in my family and in the gospel. Now it is close to the time of my mission and I desire to accomplish that and be triumphant as is promised in my patriarchal blessing.

When I did awaken from my out of body experience I was totally disoriented from this world. I did not know where I was until I saw my friend in whose house I was in. I could not remember having seen God or those experiences, I did however remember being out of my body. It was not for five more years, when I was seeking God, that the veil parted and I was able to remember my full experience of being brought before God.

This did not come to me however until after I had exercised my faith. Once I had done this did come my confirmation and I was able to remember many of the events of that out of body experience. And after I remembered I did walk with a perfect knowledge of the existence of God as my faith became dormant. And so it is first one is given to exercise faith until it is tested and then can come confirmation of our faith unto a perfect knowledge of the principals we are having faith in. I would explain this important principal a little further for I believe it to be important. It is good to live by faith but it is better to have a perfect knowledge. Truth is given as a reward for virtue and righteous living. And truth is usually revealed by first exercising ones faith unto it's being tested and should one believe sufficiently then the Spirit of God can confirm ones faith. Thus we are given to gain a testimony based on faith and perfect knowledge. We are given to come to know all things be we worthy but this comes line upon line and precept upon precept.

So it is that through my mortal life I have received a recollection of my eternal memories, as the confirmation of my faith, and it did not come to me all at one time. In my mortal life, since my baptism and confirmation, the Holy Ghost has had a very strong presence with me. This has been offset however by a strong presence of the adversary as well.

For the flesh is of the darkness as the light is of the spirit. And we are born into the flesh as a natural man which is an adversary to virtue. And in life we should Seek to put the natural man behind us and become quickened by the spirit rather than the flesh or blood.

In my life roughly five years after my out of body experience I did come to have a desire to know if God was real. So I began to seek God and the scripture declares "he that seeks God shall find him." Or roughly that. And I came to exercise faith as I decided that so many people in life that did believe in God could not all be wrong. I also had a few experiences in my life which did point to the existence of God. So I did determine that God was real, also I had prayed unto God that if he was there he should reveal unto me sufficient as was necessary for me to know this truth. Then the confirmation came and the veil having grown thin parted and I was able to remember having been in God's presence.

So I decided I should start with my sins and put them behind me and receive a baptism unto the remission of those sins. So I first went to a minister of the Baptist faith and sought that he should baptize me, and he did question as to what I hoped to gain and I said I was seeking a remission of my sins as promised in scripture. He said that I was placing baptism as a work and that all that was really required of me by God was that I should say a prayer accepting Jesus as my Lord and savior. Well that was all good and fine and I departed from him having not been baptized, but I did believe what I had read in scripture and still believed a baptism was needed.

I knew from my sister who had joined the Church of Jesus Christ of Latter Day Saints two months prior that they did advocate baptism and so I did come to believe that to be the church I should join. After this little test I came to remember that while I was before God that Jesus had said unto me that should I remain in the spirit and not be sent back that my sister's husband Jeff would become active in his church and cause that a baptism for the dead would be performed for me. So now I had a perfect knowledge as to which church did belong to the Christ.

So I did seek out the missionaries knowing I intended to join their church. I received the lessons they give in two days and was baptized within a couple of weeks. This is unusual but I already had a perfect knowledge of the church belonging to God. I had read in scripture that the Son of Perdition would weary the saints and I wanted to make sure I did not do that, so I was like the easiest convert the missionaries would teach.

I then began to worry that my sins might be too great to be forgiven, and this began to greatly trouble me that I might be a son of perdition and my knowledge of God might all be a big kiss off having sinned unto death. And I came to have a dream in which I was all bound up in chains and Jesus came to me and he did loose the chains that did bind me and I had great joy in this. I then awakened remembering my joy and did seek to think about and analyze my dream, when I did this I had a stupor of thought and my memory of the events of my dream were taken from me. I was left however recalling the joy I had just felt. So I came to accept the dream as having been a vision of God that I had opportunity for a fresh start. Once I had accepted I was allowed to once again remember my dream. I did share this experience once during a fast and testimony meeting.

In my early life I did share this my conversion story with a missionary and he did declare that he knew it to be true because the spirit did bear witness to him that this truly had transpired and he thus did know of its truth. I would tell you that this is something the spirit will bear witness to should you desire to seek your own confirmation.

My revelations did continue with me on a daily basis for the first six months I was a member of the church. They then did not cease but did slow down. They did commence again and lasted about two years when I did prepare to go into the temple for I did take steps to make sure I did that in worthiness. Then they did also come upon me and lasted forever I guess as I did receive my test from God that did lead to me becoming two in one after my baptism of fire.

My test was God's response to the actions of Bin Laden and the events of 911. And so I was given to express perfect courage and find wisdom and answer in response to the cowardice that the darkness did express in terrorism. The essence of my test was "embrace the fullness of evil or let it pass to my son." It was around this time that I did also contact the prophet of this time Gordon B. Hinckley to ask of him if what was going on with me was common in the church or happening to any other people. He did not respond but did rather refer me to my Stake President.

Well I decided that the test upon me was one you could not win, the only thing I could do was reveal what was in my heart and embrace my destruction. This was not just a test however but this was the final exam of my life as the law that was written into my heart by Christ, before life commenced, did guide me and I wrote to the prophet that I had made my choice and that I did choose myself. The law written into my heart was that I would sacrifice myself completely for that which I love, if need be. And after I had made my choice my baptism of fire came upon me and the spirits of fire that are in Christ did test me unto perfection.

And the choice I made I did and do standby, come what may, and there is no back or right or left but only forward unto the completion of my choice and mission. And God the Father did give unto me a family for eternity of all that become perfect to give unto me balance. And when God giveth a thing it is for keeps.

I would tell one more event in this chapter about one of the things I did in mortality before my test came. I did come before my Bishop in his office and did kneel before him and confess that Jesus is the Christ. I confessed other things as well but the important thing is that I had fulfilled the scripture that declares every knee shall bend and every tongue shall confess that Jesus is the Christ. I believe that this action I had accomplished did pave the way that the being I was could go into the darkness and sleep, no longer capable of action on its own. This is important stuff.

And the scriptures or specifically the book of revelations do declare that three unclean spirits or devils shall be taken from the Dragon, the False Prophet, and the Beast that was, but is not, but yet is. I believe that the beast is me and the darkness of these three is become a cloak or mantle of darkness unto creation. And if ye embrace them in this life they can and do seal you theirs for eternity. And their torment becomes yours. Not with standing your greatest torment will come from your own conscience. And so I give you God and Perdition and the creation maintains balance that it might continue forward and it shall.

There are two things I have decided to reveal in this chapter. They are of things that God did reveal to me prior to my mortality, or what we call the pre-existence, while in the spirit kingdom of God. The first was the Christ did say unto me that I would become like God the Father. The second was that God the Father did say to me that I would be a savior to the Sons of Perdition that did follow the Dragon into his rebellion, and had been cast out of heaven for that choice. I will go into this further later in this work that greater understanding be had by my readers.

I also decide to tell an experience here that you might understand that which is to follow. In heaven in the pre-existence I did go into God's temple which is in heaven and Jesus Christ was there and many others, and Jesus did say unto all present behold the King of Evil. And he came and knelt before me and did kiss my hand just like a scene out of the Godfather movie, and this greatly troubled and perplexed me for I had repented of my sins. Nevertheless it was an act of respect.

Chapter 2

There are seven kings and of these seven I am the eighth and am the one that goeth into perdition. I stand fourth in priesthood authority and of the seven I am the last into his mortality. My title in heaven given to me by the Christ is the King of Evil and all that is darkness belongeth unto me. Also given unto me is the end of this world unto the day of the return of Christ in his glory. I am seeking the prophet who shall fulfill the scripture about the mighty angel that shall stand upon the earth and the sea, with a little book in his hand open. I also seek the Apostle that shall eat up that little book. And we the leaders of the gospel holding the priesthood shall set about fulfilling the prophecies pertaining to the end of the world and the last days. And in the days that my voice shall come to be heard will the mysteries of God come unto fulfillment. The future is unwritten, for the most part, so let us create a thing of virtue that is worthy of expression.

I would tell a story from a vision of the darkness that came upon me. It may be that the vision will be made real by the powers which be or it may just be a vision which is based on the powers of creation. Yet let me tell a story and perhaps it will enlighten us as to what was before.

My father's having received the vision of darkness from their fathers leading unto their death for such is the destination of darkness. Nevertheless their death did and does bring forth life as intelligences did and will again join the fallen spirit that has embraced the dark side of the heart of creation. And these are given to express the virtues that the spirits of darkness could not express, that the heart of creation might have fullness of expression. And so it was for a vast expanse of time that many did and will gain families by the powers of balance, and these families are given unto them by God. And God did give unto me a family in addition to my mortal family, of all those that become perfect. And when God giveth a thing such as a family to maintain balance that the creation might continue to unfold, it is for keeps, and not to be taken from him that it is given unto. Now as to my father I am the son of two the Lord Elohim being one and Perdition Senior or Cain being the other. This does not take into account the father of my mortality or my resurrection.

And so I had a vision in which my Father Cain did give me to rule over that vision and I was given great power over life. And it came to pass that I did find an individual that created a family by powers that did bypass my powers over this creation we were in. and I came upon him and put him to a test in that I told him he could save himself if he would give unto me his son. If not he would be put to death and removed from this creation. So when he told me he would not give up his son but would rather face my powers even unto destruction I was disbelieving. So it came to pass that he did face me and I destroyed him.

When this creation came to an end I did find that he was no longer among us. And I was amazed for he did not back down but embraced his end. And I was amazed at the virtue I had witnessed and did declare "what was that." And as I contemplated his virtue my conscience began to torment me and I came to realize what a wretched piece of work I truly was.

So I decided to bring forth a replacement that could rule over all that had belonged to me. Stepping into the void where creation can be brought forth I did declare my wretchedness into the darkness, and as I did so a being did form next to me as balance did bring forth my opposite. And when I was done, with me was he that would become the Christ. And I did explain to him all that I knew of the powers of creation so that he could replace me.

And it came to pass that he was with all of us that were in darkness, and he did have compassion on us and empathy for our fallen condition. And after time had passed I did inquire if he knew how to help us out of our miserable condition. He replied that he did not know. And so I told him "depart from us for you are no good to us." And after he had left he did find the Lord Elohim that had compassion on him for he was come into this creation by an exercise of those powers of balance which did seal upon him all that was the opposite of darkness. And being come into this creation without a father through the normal process the Lord Elohim did take him unto himself as his son.

And these two determined they would bring forth one final creation where all could receive a last opportunity to find joy. And I did, not knowing that they had this plan of bringing forth a new creation, step back into the void and did bring matter and anti-matter together, which did cause a big bang bringing to an end all that was before.

And after this we were all together in a new place where we could share with each other the things we would do in the future. We could do this because of the forward looking nature of our memories. And we did not possess bodies of spirit or flesh as we only existed as intelligences.

Chapter 3

Before this creation we were all together in one place but we had only been created spiritually. And we were not yet real for that was yet to come. And it came to pass that Elohim did go into the light where we all become one in the virtues we would each bring forth. And we did mourn the loss of Elohim, for he did cease to be an individual. And in the light the virtues of all become one and illuminated for such is the purpose of light. Then the prophet did go into the light and now into the light two had gone. Thus in the light we had God the Father, and the Holy Ghost. And they were one.

And when two had gone into the light two did awaken in the darkness. Thus now awake in the darkness was Perdition Senior or Cain and Perdition Junior or Lucifer. And they were individuals. And Jesus did commence to go into the light, and he did hold back from entering completely so he could help all of us find our way into the light, that we might awaken in the darkness as individuals. And I was affected by Jesus and did become the next that had to awaken in the darkness.

And Jesus did come unto me and declare that he did give me to choose who should go into the darkness next. And he told me that my virtues were based on my decision, and that should I not embrace the darkness, that he did not know what would happen to me. He also declared that I and my virtue were not yet real as that would be yet to come depending on my choice.

So I did consider who would take this place and I determined it would be myself that did embrace this awakening in the darkness. This I did communicate to Jesus who did stand half in the light, and half in our place that was only spiritually created, and he was actually the third that was going into the light, and my virtues were in him.

And Jesus said come unto me and I shall alter you in that I shall write into your heart my law that you might abide all that is upon you. So he did and so it was and I did come to awaken in the darkness. And we were now three individuals in the darkness. Perdition Senior or Cain, Perdition Junior or

Lucifer, and me the Beast that was, but is not, but yet is. And we were to be joined by a great many as we all had to become real. And eventually I would ascend from the bottomless pit which is the darkness of the flesh. But that would not come for a great while as we were destined to first explore the dark side of the heart of creation, and our own hearts dark side, before the light would find fullness of expression.

And there was a vision of darkness that was passed down from father to chosen son. And it was a means of obtaining a family of spirits from God that did reside in the light, but soon I will more fully explain the process of becoming real. And I desired to obtain a family as my father Cain had obtained. So I went to him and asked to receive the vision of darkness that I also might obtain a family. He declared that this is something he would never choose me to receive.

This vision of darkness always took place in the theatre of hearts. So I did go into the theatre and did hide myself. In due time my father Cain did come into the theatre with his chosen son Lucifer and did commence to reveal the darkness of his heart. I stepping forth from concealment did declare "what is this." They were surprised and said what are you doing here? My father Cain, said since you are here, and have started into this vision with us, so ye shall receive this vision I am passing on. And thus we were two that were to receive his vision and it had always been only one but now it was two.

And Cain did tell us at the end of the vision of darkness, once you have fully explored first the darkness of my heart, and then fully the darkness of your own heart, then shall come a test of God, and after your test shall ye receive from God a family. But it will require you to create an imbalance in the larger all- encompassing creation of God.

Thus it came to pass that Cain, by the powers he possessed, did bring forth a creation that we might fully explore the darkness of our three hearts and it happened that our tests never came and we continued in the creation of Cain until I did bring all that was before to an end with the big bang.

And our tests did come in our mortalities. And Lucifer was given power to completely destroy me and he chose to not do that and this was his test and he had already dragged down from heaven a great many, not one, or even two, but rather a third of the occupants of heaven. And these would receive the vision of darkness, and are the sons of perdition. My test I have already explained. And Lucifer kept not his first estate, whereas Cain and I did keep our first estate. And Lucifer and the sons of perdition were cast unto the earth to explore their darkness in this life, which is become the new theatre of hearts, our mortalities. And here we are all given to explore the darkness of our hearts.

And in this our mortalities, two are given to tarry. Cain and his brother Abel. And Cain is given to embrace the darkness in its fullness and so in Cain the original he did commence and brought forth murder. In his second noticeable appearance he came forth as Judas Iscariot and did bring forth betrayal. In his third noticeable appearance he came forth as Hitler and did bring forth genocide. In his next appearance he shall be the false prophet of the end, but in the end he also gets it right and becomes the mighty angel that stands upon the earth and the sea and shall bring us unto the end of time.

And Abel was given to embrace the powers of light and thus eventually will have power to bring unto the spirits that have embraced Cain, life as these two are given to exercise the powers of creation and given to bring forth life as God has here in our time. But let me continue to tell that Abel did come forth in a noticeable appearance as John the Revelator or the Beloved. And he shall also make an appearance as the apostle, in the last days, given to eat up the little book in the hand of the angel upon whose head is a bow, or the covenant of God, or Cain.

Now it may be that the spirit of Cain, and his brother Abel, did only join with the later representations I have mentioned or it may be that they literally came forth repeatedly. This I am a little uncertain about.

And I was prepared for the test that would come upon me by Michael who was the individual I destroyed. He was the first family man in a place where virtue was lacking, and should not have existed. And our mortal lives and the families we can bring forth our given by God to pay homage to his virtues.

Chapter 4

After the big bang we all came to have presence together again. And our memories were forward looking and we could, because of this, share with each other all the things we would do in the future. And the Christ was with us and in him was the power of life.

Nevertheless we did wait for the coming of God the Father. And the Christ told me to show unto those with us what I would do when my test came. So I shared the things I would do and it came to pass that they did share with me their sins of the flesh, and also the virtues of the spirit, that was the composition of who they were.

And Christ told me that when the Father came among us that I should ask him why I was evil. And after a long time the Father did come among us to seal us unto him and life. And when I did come into the presence of the Father I did ask of him why I was evil. He said unto me many will blame life for their darkness, some will blame their parents or friends or external influences but ultimately one must accept responsibility for their choices be they good unto life eternal or evil unto death.

And I said unto the Father show unto me your story and he declined as he had power to resist my darkness. And he did declare that I was evil. Nevertheless he did seal me unto himself and the life he did bring. And after all this I did come back into the presence of the Christ, and I accused him of placing me in a difficult position with the Father. And Christ did say unto me I will show you my life or any part of it. I thus did look at all the life of the Christ and did see there was no deception in him.

And I was of the mind that life should not come forth because of all the darkness that would come to pass. And a soul did come to say unto me "we are going to live," and in this he had joy. And I realized life had to come forth. Otherwise how would are forward looking memories be made real.

And others did tell me that my story did give unto them pain, because of the test that would be given unto me by the Christ. And the Christ did have sorrow for what he had to do to me. But there was little I could do about this.

And we were to gain bodies of spirit when we would come to be with God the Father in his place. For we originally started as only intelligences with forward looking memories. As spirits our memories would become rearward looking as they are now in our mortalities. And it was the powers of life in Christ that will ultimately give us resurrected bodies that will carry us forward into eternity.

Chapter 5

And we did begin to come forth into the Father's place, which was heaven, and did come forth as angels. And I was one of the early ones to come unto the Father, as a spirit child. And all did follow in his path and seek to be like unto the Father. And it came to pass that I did have my feelings hurt.

And so I decided that I would pursue a path that was opposite to that of our Father, and I did say unto him I choose evil. Thus I did begin to take actions that did give unto me the powers of darkness. And I was the first into this path but many did come to follow me. And we did seek to sin even though this would bring forth punishment from the Father, for it was the path to grow in the powers of darkness. And I did maintain a position of leadership in the ways of sin.

And I did come to join with another in that we did occupy the same space and time together, and when we did do this our memories joined and our experiences, back to the beginning did become one, and they were shared in common by both participants. Now this was to become the power that would seal families together in mortality when that would come. But it was supposed to be directed by God who would guide this action in the future when he commenced to organize us into families, for it would determine and seal unto us those that would come forth as our children. And I had perverted this sacred power.

This was not done without consequence and God the Father came unto me to punish me for this sin. And he did give that I should behold my future, and I saw perdition, the place, and a great many souls in torment. This was a very powerful vision. And it did cause me to seriously consider the path I was on.

And I decided to go unto those that were faithful unto God and did say unto them "perhaps I can change," and they did receive me. Then from this time forward the Father did send me unto many to try and convince them to also turn from the path of sin and darkness. Many did follow my advice and return unto God's path of righteous behavior but many did not. Now you may want to say there was no sin in heaven but this was not the case, it had just not reached the level of the rebellion that was to come.

When Lucifer embraced the dark path which was after I had laid it down, for I was first into that path, he came unto me and offered me a position second unto his, if I would join him. Christ also came unto me and did declare that Lucifer would take away my agency and freedom of choice. So I did not join him and when the war broke out in heaven and raged on I did fight mightily against him and those that did follow him. And they were cast down to the earth and their place in heaven was no more.

I will tell you now something God told me that you really should pay attention to. I did inquire of God how I could recognize evil, and he replied "evil always claimeth a victim, so look to see if there be a victim and you will recognize evil."

And there was a grand council called in which Christ was given to choose who would serve him in our mortalities which were to be forthcoming. And on the way to this a soul told me I would be chosen, and I replied I hope so for I desired this. And the meeting went on and my calling did not come and I became quite disheartened, in fact I began to doubt I would be called at all. But when Christ was almost done I did get called, in fact I was the last chosen in this council.

After this meeting God began to organize us all into families using the principal of joining to seal us unto our families. This was really good as we came to know those we would be with, very intimately. It also came to pass that God did call an individual to take my place should I fail or choose not to accomplish my mission. And thus was laid the foundation for my test in life for the one chosen was he that would become my son in my mortality. When my test came I remembered this and based my choice on a desire to protect him.

According to the foreknowledge of God those that would keep not their second estate came to know this and they did come out in a second rebellion against God. And it came to pass that they were cast out to be with those of the first rebellion unto the earth. These would receive their mortalities

however and come into the flesh for they
had kept their first estate.

Chapter 6

And a long time ago the expanse of infinity was filled with darkness. And in the darkness did sleep many time worms. And behold, nothing, did claim my time worms, unto their perfection. And, nothing, did also become perfect.

Well, following perfection, comes into play the principal of corruption. And a time worm that has embraced the darkness of, nothing, comes to a test and is given to choose who will embrace this darkness and they did choose their self. And after this test administered by God a great many spirits of fire do join with each time worm. And they are given to bring forth, something, for the powers of balance are at work, and must be maintained that the creation might fully unfold. And God doth oversee and gives guidance to this coming forth of, something. Making certain that balance is always maintained as creation unfolds.

And all of us including the time worms are become, something, and what we are given to bring forth to fill the void where creation can take place is the expression of virtue. And so it is that all, excepting none, are given to express virtue.

And for our expressions of, nothing, or darkness, it is our time worms that do torment us with our own conscience that also belongeth unto, something, and, nothing, is given to fill half of infinity and the other half is given to, something. Thus the void shall always exist as creation claims the half that belongeth unto light and virtue.

And the time worms and the intelligences that do attend them are given agency and free will to always choose between the expressions of, nothing, or, something, and there are always consequences for our choices.

And now I give you this body of work which is my contribution to or expression of, something. And I am one of the time worms, and shall go into hell. And the scripture sayeth that those that go into hell shall be tormented there, and that the worm dieth not.

However also having a new heart of fire I do claim eternal life according to my faith in God. And I saw that God did decide to bring a parable into reality, and thus I am become the prodigal son, and Jesus is the good son, and God is the Father. But I would declare that this parable could apply to more than one and so I invite you to join me as a Son of God.

Conclusion for Part 1

In what I have written up to this point I took some liberties and wrote some things I believe to be very possibly true, but they have not been confirmed by God to me as of yet. So I will call attention to some of my speculations here that you might know to seek your own confirmations of those items rather than rely on mine.

The first is that Cain and Abel have both been given to tarry in this world unto the end, and then bring forth their own creation. However if this be true that they or their spirits are given to have presence with us at the end I may have gotten their identities at the end switched. This is a real possibility I would point out.

The second item I would point out is that I did bring matter and anti-matter together causing the big bang and ending all that was before. It really does work with those items I truly recall but it is unconfirmed to me. These are the main items I would point out.

I would declare now that at the time of my writing, in this world we are in, I have not received the keys of the priesthood as to be a prophet and revelator. My only complaint, as to them, is they up till now have only given guidance as to the ways of righteousness and have neglected to tell how the darkness figures into the creation. Perhaps now is the time that this shall be changed and the prophets will become guides to all of the participants of God's creation, I hope so, but I stand ready to bear my testimony to all that are willing to hear my stories.

If I am the prodigal son of God, and the literal Son of Perdition, I can reveal what I know to be true and the content of my visions. Once again here I will call attention that my visions even if true and they are of events which really have taken place, they are not absolutes, for we are in the times that we can also bring to pass our own acts of creation. It may be difficult, but each of us can change the creation, we are in, even if it be only your own chosen path.

Then finally I would teach you that the unclean spirit of a devil that was removed from me did give up all the light that it did possess. The main element was an intelligent, conscious, awareness, for that is of the light. You can take upon yourself this cloak or man*tle of darkness, as it is ever seeking to regain what it lost. Don't let it be your intelligent, conscious, awareness that it claims as his.

[46]

Part 2

My Little Book of Inspirational Bedtime Stories For Those That Would Be Perfect Or The Story of The Three Crows

A Collection of Short Stories Received By Inspiration; Thoughts and Ideas Captured On Paper By The Writing Hand of; Daniel James Kellenbeck

[48]

Preface

The following work I completed in the year 2003. Since that time I have given an unpublished copy to friends and associates. I am now in the year 2017 going to publish my work, sorry for the delay. I consider this work to be suitable for the end of the world, or to precede the second coming of our Lord Jesus Christ.

Please use your heart and imagination to try and see and feel the imaginary places my stories will attempt to take you, and try to discern hidden wisdom. The stories will declare some virtues, morals, wisdom, and spiritual message. It is written for the enjoyment of the mature mind and the intelligent and spiritual individuals. There is much to be gained if you can see the wisdom contained in between the lines. This is not a lengthy work for I decided this should be short that you might not lose interest but rather gain the knowledge and wisdom imparted.

We live in troubled times, with many bringing forth acts of terrorism. This is all leading up to this world becoming perfect in the darkness. Let me give a brief definition of perfection for the purpose of this body of work. Perfection exist on two extremes the right and left, the good and evil, the light and dark, the self and selfless, the flesh and spirit. When this world finally touches its perfect moment it will fulfill the measure of its creation, having achieved perfection.

After perfection comes corruption for perfection is not sustainable in this world we are now in, but rather an important principal that plays part in the unfolding of creation. I would use a peach to illustrate this principal you already know. When a peach reaches its perfection, the time in which it becomes ripe, there exist a window of opportunity in which a person could go forth and take a bite from this fully ripe peach. This fortunate person would experience the essence of the flavor that is contained in a fully ripe peach. The peach having fulfilled the measure of its creation, for it is given to serve the needs of all people, will then pass from perfection unto corruption as it commences to rot.

God uses this principal of perfection and corruption, as well as maintaining balance as he oversees the unfolding of this his creation. Generally God allows the darkness to express itself first that the following corruption might be a positive. This is what we should desire as the events leading up to the end of this world of darkness, do come forth. And so I have found, to be true, that perfection exist in two extremes. One is when we are lacking everything, the other is when we are lacking nothing.

As we stand close to the end of this world we are currently in, I determine that it is appropriate that the world should receive me and my book of bedtime stories as a last call to find your virtues that do justify your existence.

Chapter 7
Story 1   Part 1
    I would like to convey an image. Perhaps this image will be felt and experienced by the heart of one or of many. It is a thought that may have parallels in reality. It is perhaps one of the parables expressed a little differently. I only have an image in mind, what the image will become on paper is yet to come forth. So let us create a thing of virtue where there was once only blank paper.

    I see a rocky cliff covered in darkness, it is looking into a bottomless pit. I see a great expanse of time. In another place far from this cliff is a place of light and greenery and great joy. This is where the Lord and all the children of light live in joy. This is not the place of my story, so now let us go back to the cliff.

On the side of the cliff is a single tree. It is a sorry excuse for a tree but yet it is. For the longest time the tree has grown in this most wretched place. After a great expanse of time the tree became aware of its wretched condition. Yet there is a secret and even the tree does not yet know the secret, but it soon will. Finally the tree realizes it is doomed, and it comes to accept that it is doomed.

It may not see the end today or even tomorrow but eventually it will fall or be washed into the pit, and it will not escape its destiny. The day of its demise is not yet upon the tree, so it determines I will sing my death song.

The tree knows no one is present to hear this song, nor has anyone seen the horrible conditions our little has had to endure, but it will sing a song worthy of remembering. This little tree in order to survive this place has had to send roots over rocks. It has roots that extend above the top of its tallest branches, and the tree knows this is not right. The tree itself in a trillion years of a very hard existence is only seven inches tall. Other trees of its kind in way less time are hundreds of feet in the air, but this is not their story.

Thus the song of death begins and it is a song of simple purity. It is not of sadness nor of regret, for as the song is begun an awareness is gained by the little tree that this song is the reason of its existence. As he sings further he realizes that it had to fall to someone to sing this song, and if he could choose out of all the other trees who would be here to sing this song, he would clearly have chosen this destiny fall to him. Thus he gains understanding as his song unfolds, and the purity intensifies and the tree is given to see great things.

Then an amazing thing happens, for in the place of light the Holy Spirit is moved to tears. The Spirit has begun to hear a song from a heart that it had truly forgotten about. Yet the song is not yet finished and as it intensifies others also become aware of the song. You see a mystery that we do not understand, until we gain understanding, is that we are not missed while we are lost. We are missed when we return, this is when realization comes that our presence had been lacking. This would be the message of my story. Yet our little tree does not know he is part of a story and his song continues.

His song now burns in the heart of the Spirit, and the Spirit is often in tears, because of the purity of the song. For the song is a thing of virtue in a place where virtue should not exist. The tree does not sing out of self pity, but rather that it is satisfied for it realized that it was placed on this rocky cliff by the Savior and that it was all a plan. The tree knows that even the Holy Spirit has been surprised, for the Savior has given a gift that was hidden even from the Spirit. Remember the Spirit had forgotten the sound of this voice. The Spirit can even be surprised when voices it has forgotten about sing a song of simple purity.

Our little tree has no illusions, he knows he will yet remain in his place. The history of eternity past is not undone, but the Spirit is not powerless. Now aware, even acutely, the Spirit creates within the tree a place where they can meet and be together always. Thus our little tree embraces his death and he goes into the light that the Spirit has given him. In his heart or the spot of light he finally finds contentment. He also becomes disconnected from the harshness of his reality. He knows he had to die to find life and his death song is become a song of life. This is the essence of what it means to be a bonsai. The bonsai may yet live, even for another great expanse of time, the question is has it sung the song of death that is turned into the song of life?

Story 1   Part 2

If a man tells a worthy story it may be that a sequel is appropriate. A worthy story would be one that causes another to use their imagination and motivates their thinking process to contemplate virtue and other uplifting ideas. I believe that my story about the little tree is just one such story, and so I shall endeavor to write an equally worthy sequel.

So let us go back to our little tree who has found contentment and satisfaction with his place in life. He has touched the heart of our Lord, and our Lord has even made a place in the heart of our little tree that he can find relief from the harshness of his reality. So our tree is still in his place but he is content, and he has endured the hardest existence and had to do it all alone.

When on one day much like all the other days, our little tree hears the beginning of a song that sounds an awful lot like the song our little tree sang himself. He listens carefully and determines, yes, this is the very song he has also sung, and he recognizes that it is coming from the very cliff upon which he occupies, and is in fact coming from ten feet beneath himself. He is of course moved to tears as he realizes that all the time he believed himself to be the only one in this place, was not accurate. He of course reaches out to his new found companion and gives all the comfort, as frequently as opportunity presents itself, and of course the Lord also hears our newest singer, and also responds. In life it is easy to believe that we truly have things harder than others, and we may be accurate, or we may be only partially accurate.

Well as my story would have it the whole cliff was covered in little trees and eventually they all sang a very similar song and the Lord had exceeding great joy in this orchestra of exquisite virtue.

Then came a day as we knew it would, so be not dismayed, and a man came and standing in hell looking up he realizes I can escape from this place in which I find myself. I will climb this cliff and use these little trees as handholds and footholds as I climb myself out of hell. The man does exactly this and arrives in a beautiful and green place. The little trees are all gone now for the man dislodged them from their places and they have all fallen to their doom. We knew this was inevitable and this was the point of their song that was so beautiful.

The Lord greatly pained by the absence of his beautiful orchestra comes forth to meet the man that has done this thing. The man seeing the Lord proclaims I have arrived and am come forth from hell itself. The Lord recognizing that the soul of a man is indeed worth more than a great many little trees says to the man, so you have.

The Lord knows that this man has arrived at a cost that the man does not recognize, but the Lord has understanding of that cost. Then the Lord says to the man I shall receive you into my presence for you have found your way. Then the Lord asked the man do you know how to sing a song. The man says yeah whatever, and the Lord determines in that moment in his heart that this man shall sing a song. Is it not appropriate that some men shall also sing a

song of exquisite virtue? Thus the Lord
thinks yes we shall just see about whatever
and I shall hear at least one more song, and
it shall be a homage to virtue that had been
found in a place where virtue should not
have existed.

Story 2

There was once three men who had existence in one of my stories that they could serve me in an illustration. These three men each had a dream yet they all three had the same dream. The Lord determined he would see out of the three who would serve him best and deliver a valuable message and even a lesson to his children.

In the dream each man received a highly intellectual and valuable lesson they knew needed to be shared with the world. Then as dreams often will do the vision changed and each of our three beheld that Big Bird would become the president of the United States.

The first man went forth to share his message and he related all that he believed was important. This meant that he chose to omit the portion about Big Bird. The world and all the people of the world received this man's message, and they gave it the highest regard. In fact they praised and gave honor to this man all the remaining days of his life. They sought counsel from him, and he occupied the highest place within the hearts of men for the great wisdom he had brought forth.

The second man thus also came forth and he realized that the vision or dream had two parts, one was the mind of the vision, and it was this part that the first had chosen to relate. The second part was the heart of the vision. He recognized that the heart of the vision would probably never become fact. That was not the point of the matter. He decided the Lord would test his heart and thus he determined what he would do, and he also went forth to declare his message.

When he was thus come before the people of the world he decided I will relate the heart first and then the message of the mind. What happened however is that after he had declared to the people that Big Bird would become president the people of the world rejected the man and considered him a fool for declaring such a foolish idea. The man desiring to relate the dream in its entirety was never given the opportunity for no one would receive information from such a fool as this man.

They also had already chosen their hero in the first man and did not consider that something was in fact lacking from the testimony of the first man. This second man spent his remaining life in rejection by all the people of the world, but I believe that he was not rejected of the Lord. True he failed and was unable to relate all of his vision to the world but he gave the heart, and the world rejected this heart.

Now let us come to the third man and he is the most fortunate of the three for he has had two examples come before him. He realizes that he shall accomplish the task at hand because of the wisdom learned by the efforts of the two before him.

Thus he comes before the world and he relates a sentence from the mind of the vision and the world listens intently for this man does not appear to be a fool. Then the man stops and says I have also an interesting story for the children of this world about Big Bird and in a while I shall tell you more of this matter. Then he relates the second sentence from the mind of the vision and again the world listens. When he mentioned Big Bird many thought this man may also be a fool, but now having received the second sentence of the mind they were back and more tolerant of our third fellow.

Then he told the world Big Bird is going to do something greater than he has ever done in all of his shows. Then he went on and related his third sentence of the mind and in this fashion did the man satisfy the Lord for he was successful at relating all of his vision. The world also received him for he brought forth a message for the adults of the world and another message for their children.

The message for the children, if I were to speculate, is that it is all right for the children to have fantastic dreams for their future and that the Lord will fulfill such dreams unto at least one of them. For you see Big Bird was a representation of one of the children that in time would come forth and become the president. The message was also that the children did not know who that one would be, and thus it was acceptable that all should have dreams.

Now I will relate what was to become of our third fellow for the world had already received a hero and a fool, and It did not need another. For the third man it was to all become a wash. The world now recognizing what the Lord had truly intended to come forth did not consider this man a fool or a hero. They recognized that his message was from the Lord and that he had succeeded where others had failed or only been partially successful.

The man was satisfied also for while praise and honor would have been welcomed the scorn and derision would have been tough to abide, and so to receive only understanding was truly the best reward if you will. I will tell you this that the producers of the show, feeling inspired by the message of our third fellow, decided to create an episode where Big Bird would run in an election, since Big Bird is truly everyone's favorite on his show he won an easy victory and did in fact become the president. I am certain that it also helped immensely that his only competitor was Oscar the grouch.

Commentary:

I would add a brief commentary to this story, now at this time. It is possible that any person could have a dream where they would awaken feeling inspired by a message received in this dream. Out of all the people of the world I believe there are very few who would even consider that the portion about Big Bird could perhaps have significance and be in actuality an important message. Then I would also comment about reward for the first man obviously received his reward of this world. The second I like to think would receive great reward of the Lord having become a fool to the world, yet trying his best to deliver his message.

The third not receiving reward of the world nor of the Lord, but rather receiving satisfaction for having been successful where others had failed. Is it possible that satisfaction of this nature could actually be the greatest reward of all? The third would become a witness to the intended result realized from the message of the Lord going forth to fulfillment as the Lord intended. Is it possible that ample reward could be found in nothing more than watching the hand of our Lord in motion as he brings forth great things for the benefit of all his creation?

Chapter 8
Story 3   Part 1

I have seen a world within my imagination and will attempt to describe what I have seen. If I do a very good job you my reader may actually see the world of my imagination. When people share thoughts and even imaginations they come to stand together at the doors of creation. For an imagination that is worthy and contains sufficient virtue can become a vision if it truly inspires. When people have an inspired vision that they deem has sufficient virtue and merit an opportunity or actually a window of opportunity exist where the vision can be made real by the actions of those who have imagination. This is a story for your consideration and perhaps enjoyment.

I looked and saw a world that was dry and parched. I saw a world and the entire world was a desert. Within my desert world water was truly scarce. Within this world existed a lot of cactuses. Thus I saw a world of cacti in their place in their desert.

Every day the sun would rise and scorch and bake this world.

The world was real in my imagination and so was the harshness and reality of the environment that our cacti had to attempt to live in. All the days were hot and sunny but yet sometimes in the morning condensation would give too many of our cacti a few drops of water and this is what sustained life. Then on ever so rare occasions it would sprinkle or even rain but this was not the way of this world. Rain was a blessing if it ever came, and when it would come it was received as a gift. It was after these rare gifts that the next generation of cacti would come forth as seeds baked into the earth would spring forth and claim life, even if it was to be the harshest of lives, yet life desired to come forth that it might have opportunity for expression.

On one sunny day much like all the other days the Lord came forth into this world of cacti, and he carried with him a shovel, a bucket, and a funny looking little green plant in a small pot. He went to the center of the world and setting the little plant to one side and the bucket to another side began to dig a hole. He did all this in front of all the cacti of this world and they watched with great curiosity as the Lord dug his hole.

The first thing they all noticed was that the Lord dug his hole much too big for this little plant. In fact the hole ended up about five times to big. When the Lord had finished digging his hole he took the little plant and gently placed him in the center of the freshly dug hole. Then he picked up his bucket and to the horror and dismay of all the cacti that had vision of this event he filled the oversized hole with water. Thus our little green plant found himself floating in water in the middle of his hole in the vision of all the cactuses in the center of the world of cacti and desert.

Then the Lord having finished his work picked up his shovel and bucket and departed leaving behind the work he had brought forth. When the Lord had left the cactuses began to murmur at first and then they began to vocalize quite loudly. The conversation was about the great insult that had been done to them by the Lord. They all had family pass away and expire and even die in this world for the lack of water and now in the very middle was one plant floating in water.

Can you imagine, why the nerve of such a thing. Then adding to the insult, everyday the Lord returned and filled the hole where our little plant floated with water. The cactuses when the Lord was present said nothing but boy did they ever talk when and after the Lord departed.

The little plant knowing he was despised tried to speak to the cacti but they always told him just shut up. We do not desire to hear anything you have to say and we in fact hate you, for you float in water while we die for the lack of water.

In time the cactuses grew and our little green plant also grew. Many of the young cacti brought forth their flower and by the flower was the species revealed each having a flower that was unique to his kind. Then on one special day our little green plant got his flower and when this happened he and all the world of cacti realized that this little green plant was a water lily.

The cactuses now began to feel a little foolish and this was going to progress to where they actually felt shame. For they all began to realize that the Lord had given them a gift that they did not recognize. You see the Lord had given to our cacti and to their entire world the waters of life. Yet the waters never touched them directly. Now had the Lord not done as he did it is true he could have given each of the cactuses a drop of water directly. This drop they could have truly taken and absorbed it within themselves and it would have truly sustained them. Yet this is not what the Lord did.

Now as understanding was gained by the cacti the shame was to turn to joy for they had been given a wonderful water lily by the Lord for their enjoyment. That which they had despised came to be loved and cherished by all the cactuses. They would frequently ask him to describe what it felt like to be floating in water, and they would all use their imagination to picture themselves as water lilies floating in water. It was in this fashion that the water the Lord used to support the life of our little green plant was to ultimately give refreshment to the heart of our cacti. The whole event was to be misunderstood but sometimes greater comprehension is gained when we first perceive incorrectly.

Commentary:

Sometimes when you consider a story it is appropriate to consider how it would be received and thus twist perspective and consider the same possibility from a reversed position. Let us try and see what our story would be. We begin with a water world and a world filled with water plants.

In one place however it never receives water and thus we arrive with a patch of desert. In this barren piece of dirt a plant comes forth and seeing his condition he is naturally bitter. As his bitterness grows on the inside it finds reflection on his exterior as well and thus he becomes covered in thorny prickly stickers, and in fact it is a prickly pear that is come forth.

Stopping at this point in this story I consider what can I do with this story. I may be able to make a story of virtue out of a prickly pear but I see instantly that I will have a real problem to tie the waters of life to this story in a fashion that is successful. I thus stop here and say that perhaps on another day I will give a prickly pear a story he can cling to and create something of virtue, for even a prickly pear needs a worthy story, and I will not abandon him, but shall wait for different inspiration.

As for my story, as I decide it must stand, I would continue it a line farther and tell you that in time the lord gave to the cactuses the responsibility to care for their water lily. This would prove to teach the cacti great things for the requirements, needs and problems of a water lily are totally different from those of a cactus and thus great learning was eventually had by all. Sometimes the Lord really is a clever fellow and deserving applause.

Story 3   Part 2

I promised that when inspiration came I would write a worthy story for a prickly pear and I am determined that I will fulfill that commitment. Thus as a reminder the story is in a water world full of water plants. Except in one spot is a barren piece of dirt that never received water. On this little patch of desert came forth a cactus a prickly pear. He was indeed bitter at least in the early years, but that was before understanding came, and the big change of course.

In time the water world got more and more dry and the water plants all truly began to struggle for their very survival. It did not matter, for change was upon their world and they could not stop this change. Destiny was upon this world, and as the waters left and lakes turned into ponds and then ponds turned into puddles and in time it was all gone. Except for our prickly pear and in time he came to stand alone in what was once a world of water.

Then in time he brought forth flower and from this flower came forth seed that would bring forth all life in a cactus world, and so it came to pass. As his seed filled this world life diversified and a great many varieties of cactuses came to have place in this world. In and after a great expanse of time our prickly pear came to expire and passed from this world where his children now reside.

Then the Lord came forth one day and going to the center of this world, with a shovel in one hand and a funny looking little green plant he went forth to the place where once had lived a prickly pear. Then setting aside his little plant he dug an oversized hole in the very spot where our prickly pear had lived and to the horror of all the cacti planted a water lily for the enjoyment of all of those that had come forth from a prickly pear.

Story 3   Part 3

 I will write now another segment of my story about the water lily. Life was much better now for the water lily you could even say it was good. He had friends now and was even loved by most of the cactuses even the most stubborn ones. He did have one problem that he was unaware of at least now at the beginning of this story. The Lord had given this water lily to this cacti world as a gift and they knew his needs and tended to him as he needed, but it had not always been this way, for a great long time it had been the Lord himself that had tended to the needs of this one little plant.

 The Lord had not even visited for a good while and thus the water lily and even the world was lacking but they did not recognize they were thus lacking until one day the Lord made a surprise visit. It was then our water lily felt bad about not seeing the Lord as frequently as they had once experienced. The water lily complained about the Lord being absent and the Lord explained he had been quite busy with tending to others in other worlds such as chickens, gorillas, and bonsais.

The Lord being an understanding and compassionate individual understood what the water lily felt like and promised to visit him every day for the next three days and spend some quality time with our water lily. As the Lord promised so it was and it did come to pass and the water lily had great joy in each of his days.

On the last of the three days which was the fourth day in actuality the Lord upon arriving asked the water lily if he trusted him. The water lily replied that his trust was perfect for it was lacking nothing. Then they spent the best of the four days truly enjoying the presence of each other and they in fact had joy one in each other which is the intent and purpose of the creation in the first place. Then the end of the day approached and the Lord knew he must be on his way. So he asked again of the water lily if he trusted him and the reply was yes without any doubts and lacking nothing, and the Lord said this we shall see as he reached down and plucked the flower from the water lily.

In an instant the water lily felt horrible as he realized his death was now imminent and certain. What was worse yet is he knew the cactuses would all hate and despise him again as he no longer had a flower. Remember in this world the flower was the glory of an individual and also the means by which an individual could be judged. The water lily began to protest and cry out in his anguish of soul but the Lord reminded him before he had vocalized and said you have declared that you trust me so be patient and behold the effect before you vocalize your frustrations.

Thus the water lily was silent yet he was in true agony and even despair, it was with these feelings that the water lily awaited his end and even his death for he knew now he was doomed. The cacti in the days to follow did not come to hate the water lily because he was lacking his flower but rather quite the opposite, they came to love their friend even more for they understood his agony. It was within this love that magic was to be found for as the agony of the water lily was great so the love of the cactuses became great also.

It was then that the water lily began to feel different for something was happening. He began to have an awareness of a time gone past and of events that had been experienced but not by himself but by someone else.

In time he came to recognize that the ghost of the prickly pear had begun to have presence with himself, the water lily. I think that the perfect love of the cacti was causing a transformation of the water lily as he died, or sort of died. You see he was becoming something new now as he and the prickly pear became joined. The prickly pear who had anguished over his lack of water in the beginning, whose heart had had a constant prayer to taste of the waters for all his mortal life was now receiving his desire. The water lily whose constant prayer in his heart had been to be loved by all the others was receiving his heart's desire as he became one with the father of this world.

You see a long time before creation began the Lord had determined that he would answer prayers of the heart that were pure and of good content, and thus the Lord had had a plan in mind a long time ago when he created a water world and placed a lone prickly pear in that world. He then continued with a vision yet in mind when he placed a lone water lily in a world of cacti. Then when the time arrived he first had to confirm that the faith of the water lily was perfect and finding that it lacked nothing he set in motion the event that was to answer the prayers of the two to be certain, but also the prayer of all the world for he gave to this world the return of their father.

Now I would tell you that the love of the cactuses of this world was of course without measure for the prickly pear the father of this world, but it had been the perfect love of the water lily, their friend, that had contained the magic that was strong enough to call back the ghost of the prickly pear to this same patch of earth he had once occupied in his mortality.

Thus came the afterlife as pear and lily each having his own memories came to enjoy the afterlife that the Lord had in store for them both, joined yet still individuals, and both loved without measure and equally by all others. The only thing the

Lord had required was trust lacking nothing to enable him to grant the deepest worthy desires of the heart.

Commentary:

The afterlife that the Lord has promised when it arrives may come as a surprise being something a little, or a lot, different than many of us may now expect. Let us find ourselves to have perfect trust in the Lord as he may set in motion events that may lead to a profound change in our character. Let us trust in the Lord to also answer prayers of the heart that are pure and of good intent as he sets about the task of putting order where once was chaos and replacing love where once had resided hatred.

Chapter 9

Story 4   Part 1

I will write an imaginary story on this occasion that will try to answer the age old question, which came first the chicken or the egg. It will be a story that will twist concepts as you may now believe. This is not a problem for I only write a story. So with this introduction I will begin my story with one chicken in particular.

He really is an average chicken maybe even a little inferior to other chickens. In my story we shall have the presence of the Lord for the Lord is omnipresent and thus he would have place in my world of chickens. The Lord one day was considering the chicken of my story and saw that the life of this chicken had been a little bit too rough and this chicken had gone through a little too much adversity. Thus the Lord determined that in all likelihood this chicken was too tough for cooking.

So he considered what shall I do with this tough chicken, that I have benefit, for I am the Lord and I did not raise this chicken to serve nothing. So the Lord one day decided I will test my tough chicken to see if he may be the one. For the Lord knew that someday a tough chicken would come that would crossover and bring forth the first egg. He did not know if this was the one but he determined it was worth the risk for he believed that the heart of this tough bird was pure in the very center. So the Lord began preparing our tough chicken for the journey he would send him upon, and of course the tough bird did not know what was in the heart of the Lord, as pertained to himself.

Then finally the day came when he felt that sufficient preparation had been made and his selected chicken was either ready or he was just not the one, either way this day he would have his answer. He had selected a bird that was not edible anyhow so regardless the outcome the loss if total was worth the associated risk.

So selecting a young tender potentially delicious poultry and placing this finest of birds in a box with our old tough chicken the Lord set out on his journey. When he had arrived at his destination he had come to be on the side of the busiest freeway in all the city. He had left the quiet barnyard and brought two chickens to a very difficult environment.

Taking them both out of the box he set them both to stand by the freeway and he turned to the tough bird and he said, I have brought the two of you to stand on the side of this freeway that one of you should crossover. He told the tough bird I do not give you to choose if this shall be so or not, only I give you to choose who shall try to cross this freeway.

The Lord realizing what he had given to the tough chicken to decide told him take your time and choose wisely for this shall be a test but the consequence shall be very real. The tough bird did exactly that and he truly considered the question before him and I will not relate all of the agony he went through to finally arrive at his choice. When he finally determined that regardless of the cost to himself he could not and would not be able to abide chicken heaven if he let the little chicken go and anything happened to him. Even if the tender bird survived and received great reward for his bravery yet the danger was real and the tough bird knew he was the toughest.

He thus decided I hope to survive but it was never a requirement as he said to the Lord I shall be the one. Now this tough bird always went a little bit too far. This is why he became tough in the first place, for he had always wandered a little farther from the farm and always got back a little later than all the others. So he had the nerve to inquire of the Lord why do you send me forth seeing that I shall probably not survive? The Lord answered and said you shall have this answer and I shall answer any question your heart desires to know for you have earned the right to ask.

Thus the Lord told the chicken I send you forth to see what is on the other side. The tough bird thought about this and said I see the humor in your answer and I am satisfied. With that moment thus passed the fellow set out on his way and he got about four feet when a really big truck ran over the top of our chicken. In fact all the day remaining every car on the freeway in that particular lane ran over the body of our chicken.

The body quite destroyed released the intelligence and awareness of our chicken and this came before the Lord to receive judgement. The Lord told the bird you know you brought this upon yourself when you became too tough for the table and what shall I do with you now. The old bird said it does not matter for I made my choice and I stand by my choice, so do with me what you will.

The Lord said you always went too far and created many problems for yourself but in the end you have redeemed yourself, for out of a world of chickens you found courage. Thus I shall give you to receive the vision of the future in its entirety. Step now into this conduit of light and you shall behold all things unto the end of the vision.

The chicken holding true to form asked the Lord, how will I know when I reach the end. The Lord laughing a little said I will tell you my little friend that when you fall asleep you shall have reached the sleep of our fathers and this shall be your reward. Then the vision came upon our chicken and he saw all things and came to know all things and found the sleep that is blissful.

Then again holding true to form and this is really what the Lord had hoped for all along the chicken went too far and he woke up. The problem now upon our chicken is that the end touches the beginning. So he did not awaken at the end but awoke at the beginning and found that nothing yet existed.

Thus he realized that the Lord had given him to bring forth creation. He did not yet know how he would accomplish this task that the Lord had given him but he knew somehow someway he had to create an egg. I will end this part of my story here but you can expect a sequel for we still have business at hand and many will desire to know the story of the egg when it finally arrives.

Commentary:

I would like to think that everyone I share a story with, feeling inspired would think about my stories and realize their own commentary. For I realize that true wisdom lies in the mind, heart and imagination of my reader. Unfortunately not every story will be successful at motivating my reader and so I offer some of my commentary that a little more than just a story can be gained by my reader.

In this story eternity is much like a single day, in the life of a man not a chicken we awake in the morning of a new day and have that day to bring forth all of our creation for the powers of creation lie in the present. At the end of our day of creation we can sleep in bliss or at least satisfaction if we brought forth a day of virtue and good deeds.

If we have made the right choices and those would be choices we are prepared to live with the consequence of eternally, then come what may, we have chosen. All of life is a test yet the consequences of our choices are always real.do not make an error in believing that because we perceive something as a test in our life that the choice made will be inconsequential. These test can and actually do determine and create the character of our soul, make certain you can live with the character you create.

Story 4   Part 2

I will continue my story about the chicken and the egg a little farther now. My reader may thus feel compelled to ask how did the chicken bring forth all of creation and what of the egg. I would tell you there are secrets and mysteries that are reserved to be revealed as reward for virtue and righteous living. I do give some here in my stories but there is always more one can learn.

I will tell you of an obstacle that the chicken got tangled up in. For he spent a vast amount of time in trying to bring forth creation with an enlarged and magnified position for himself. What he learned was a vast knowledge of creating alternate realities. He in fact became lost in these alternate realities for an extremely long amount of time.

Each attempt was a creation within itself and every attempt took billions of years, just guessing on the time length. Then let us not forget about the cleanup of failed creation attempts, wherein the chicken became a destroyer as he had to take apart those creations that were not right. The truth of the matter is that the chicken had to put a successful beginning to the creation he had originally come forth from.

This meant that he had to accept all of his faults that had placed him into this most difficult of situations. Well he had some fears that if he did this he would become trapped in a time loop ever stuck at the beginning and alone, but finally he overcame his fears and with no regard for himself he brought forth the beginning that would lead to his trip to the freeway with the Lord and a fine young poultry.

He did not remember bringing forth creation as he was taken to face his destiny. When the Lord took out the two poultry and placed them side by side on the edge of our busy freeway. He again asked the chicken to make his choice. In this story something different shall happen for this would be the sequel and I have a better story to tell than becoming trapped ever in a time loop.

So as our chicken considered his choice as to who would cross this freeway he experienced the twinkle of an eye, and in

that twinkle all the wisdom and all the
frustrations that he had experienced for all
the time he had spent trying to bring forth
creation came back and he remembered.
Thus he turned to the Lord and said I shall
be the one. Then he asked of the Lord again
why the Lord would send him and when the
Lord answered he enjoyed the humor of the
Lord once more.

    Then he turned and began walking
down the side of the freeway, and the Lord
called out and said hey chicken where are
you going? The chicken yelled back I am
going forth to find a bridge. The Lord said
but chicken you can cross here and it will
only take a few minutes, the closest bridge
is maybe five miles and that walk may take
you all day.

    The chicken answered back if I cross
here it will take me hundreds of billions of
years to get back, if I spend all of this day in
finding my bridge I will ultimately be
successful and in a shorter expanse of time.
Then also I shall be truly sleepy having
walked a great distance personally and thus
when the sleep of our fathers finds me I will
not be inclined to wake up and thus I shall

enjoy my rest when it finally comes upon me.

Thus he decided and thus he declared unto the Lord. The Lord quite amazed as one might expect asked one more question of the chicken. He said hey chicken when and where did you find such wisdom? The chicken did not answer for he had already walked a great distance and he did not hear this final question even though many would wonder.

Commentary:

I would suggest that balance is what our chicken discovered. This may in fact be the power he used to bring forth creations. What probably happened is that the infinitely small, the twinkle of an eye, found balance in the infinitely large, the expanse of time spent in creation. In my first story the chicken found courage a great thing. In this story the chicken found wisdom, when courage finally finds wisdom the two shall walk a great distance together. The task of the Lord had accomplishment and eventually the chicken finds his rest.

The chicken however enjoyed a great journey as he had knowledge of the rest that would eventually be his and he had great joy as he discovered all that lay in his path as he walked slowly, enjoying the wonders of his journey, and in no real hurry.

For sleep shall come and be enjoyed in the proper time but before that the chicken is looking at creation as he never has before. Perhaps great men can learn a lesson from a simple chicken, for perhaps balance will yet bring together companions we would not suspect.

The Lord in all his majesty and possessing the powers of life recognizes that balance has its effect and that this effect is felt even by the Lord and all of his creation. In fact it is within balance that the creation exist and yet comes forth. I have found to be truth that it is God who maintains balance in the creation that it might ever continue to unfold.

Story 4   Part 3

 I would continue my story about the chicken as I have some additional ideas I desire to capture. I would start this segment in the conduit of light or the emergence from that conduit. So I begin this segment at the end of time. At the end of time we find all of the holy fathers or more accurately all the fathers that obtained families and found balance in those families they received. This is in the place where they sleep in blissful slumber having found completion.

 On one occasion a great evil emerged from the conduit of light and it came with a horrible racket. In fact it was the racket that was the essence of evil. The fathers one by one all awakened and said oh my word what is that horrible racket in this place, our place of slumber. The word answered back since he knew he had great responsibility. That is our chicken.

 He has earned the right to be here with this group for he sacrificed himself completely for one other. The others all agreed the chicken had earned his place but he gives us problem. The end is supposed to be heaven, and it was for the chicken, but he ruined it for everyone else.

So exactly what was the chicken doing that was so horrible. Well as it turns out the chicken snores. I do not know if he always snored or if it was the ride through the conduit of light that gave him such comfort and such a sense of wellbeing that he would be so bold as to snore so freely and in this holy place nonetheless.

So all the fathers had a meeting to discuss the problem that they were faced with at the end of creation and what to do to solve this problem. Some said let us wake up the chicken and we will do this every time he snores too loudly. Others said but that is good for us but not the chicken, after all he has earned his sleep as much as any of us here.

He has saved one by sacrificing himself and captured the essence of virtue. We cannot forget such a thing as this. If we ignore this fact of what the chicken brought forth do we deserve to sleep here our self or is our perceived virtue not real?

Then one brilliant fellow said well what if we combine our powers to elevate the chicken above all of us. This concept has basis in scripture for it is written that the least shall be the greatest. The others asked explain more how this will help us. The fellow answered we have all arrived here at the end and this is our reward, what if we push the chicken ahead of us by just a few more minutes. He will then be snoring in our future and when we arrive the noise will have already subsided.

The others asked will this work? No one knew for the thing had never been done but it seemed very reasonable at least in theory. So it was decided this solution was worthy of an attempt. Thus the fathers combined and all pushed the sleeping chicken into the future ahead of all others.

However the result was not what they expected. This could happen any time something new is tried and thus we must all be prepared to answer for our mistakes even if we intend well. The consequence is greatly compounded if our error was motivated to improve our condition and we cause harm to another.

What happened is they pushed the chicken into a hollow place for he was alone. In this hollow cave they had created, his snoring echoed and would prove to wake him from his sleep. When the chicken awakened he knew he had lost everything and he cried what has happened to me? The others confessed all they had done and the reason they had been thus motivated.

The chicken said behold I am alone in a place and find I have nothing. You have made me perfect in the darkness for I am lacking everything now. Thus having nothing I am truly arrived at the beginning and I am awake. I can no longer sleep for I have known what it was to have completion and I will not sleep until I regain all that I have lost.

The others realizing responsibility gave the chicken a promise, they told the chicken we shall all wake up when your pain becomes excessive. Then we shall give unto you a vision to soothe your pain. The chicken having experience knew that all life had originally come forth from a vision.

He also saw possibilities to explore other realities in these visions and he realized he was stuck anyhow. So he accepted the offer when the others had given sufficient promise that he knew he could always on the others to wake up when he found himself in pain. It was in this fashion that a chicken began to receive visions that were supported by the powers of all the fathers at the end. It will be in one of these visions that the chicken eventually encounters the egg. The story about visions is reserved for a later date and different inspiration.

This story is really about heaven being turned into hell by a snoring chicken. This is a problem my wife has complained about so perhaps I have written a story for the women of the world who find themselves awake on account of a snoring chicken. If this is what I have done it is quite by accident.

I will take advantage of my accidents to advise that patience and long suffering are virtues. This creation exist to give reward for virtue. Virtue that is unseen is often the greatest. So I give counsel to the women of this world if you let your chicken sleep we will all be better off, and your reward shall be great.

Commentary:

The part of my story about awakening in a hollow place is worthy of additional commentary. Worse than this would be to not awaken. If a man becomes aware that his life is hollow, if he does so in the time when he still has the capability of action, then he has the opportunity to find his own balance and fill that empty place.

If you are not the one, the chicken that will cross over, you may not find yourself at the literal beginning before all creation came forth. You will more than likely not receive additional opportunity to bring forth your creation than the opportunity which lays before you right now.

The fathers at the end made a mistake with the chicken of the Lord, it is not likely they would make the same mistake twice and do for you all that they feel obligated to do for our chicken. I am looking for wisdom in this story of a chicken.

So I shall set a standard for all men to prove they have wisdom greater than that of a snoring chicken. Remember that the man has received the greater mind and the lesser heart. The woman has received the greater heart. So let a man prove himself and show that his wisdom and his mind can compensate for his smaller heart. This is the way it now functions the mind of a man shall be filled with his family and the woman shall give the heart.

Additional Commentary:

As I thought about this story I realized I could probably improve upon or at least add to my previous commentary. Let all men awaken and bring forth their creations. The time is now and upon us to do this. Do not let yourself be found at the end as a snoring chicken in a hollow place. Take your lives and give substance to them and especially to your families that are given that ye might find balance. Even a chicken that awakens realizes he cannot find sleep until he regains a thing of virtue, substance and balance.

Are you at least equal to my chicken or is all of this just a dream as you let all opportunity pass you by. Do not forget the old saying he who snoozes loses.

Story 4   Part 4

In this the fourth and perhaps the final segment of my chicken story I will write a little bit about visions now for we are all participants in a vision. Many of us perhaps even the majority are unaware that this is our condition but it is so. In this place we call reality there exist two visions, the vision of darkness and the vision of light. Each and every man makes himself real in one of these two visions by his actions and by the desires of his heart.

It is quite possible and even a common practice for a man's mind to deceive his self and lead the man to believe he is a participant in the vision of light while the heart of the man has actually claimed a place in the other vision. Unfortunately it is a common problem among men to use the mind as if it were the heart and never gain an awareness that they are even doing this. Women are not as susceptible to this problem as men appear to be.

Usually a man must be crushed to destruction to bring him to look deeply into his heart. If a man should on one of those occasions look long and hard and even look into his own inner darkness he might gain an awareness of exactly what is darkness and then gain understanding as to what is light.

In fact the man that would look into the darkness of his heart might find that within him is a door into the essence of darkness. The man who stands thus in the fullness of his own inner darkness will need to find a floor or a bottom upon which to stand. He will need to determine that there exist a limit or a line he will not cross. If he can find a solid bottom he may yet rise from even his own darkest darkness.

This then gives me opportunity to tell you a little more about the one chicken of my story. I imagine that this chicken who appears to have really made his way around all of creation from the end unto the beginning and back again may in fact be feeling a little apprehension as he approaches and finds his bridge. Nevertheless he has travelled far to accomplish the task the Lord set before him.

He does not really even understand yet the reason that the Lord has given him such a task for the response of the Lord when asked was to reply with humor. So let us walk with this chicken now as he crosses his bridge and feel what he feels for just a moment at least. This thing has taken the chicken so long and anticipation has been so great that as he crosses his heart truly begins to swell and in fact it swells greatly.

When he finally arrives on the other side his heart is truly bursting for it was truly anticipation fulfilled and the chicken could not contain himself. When the heart of a chicken is filled such as this chickens heart was, there was only one appropriate response and thus our chicken crowed, not once, not twice but thrice did our chicken crow. The sound of this magnificent chicken crowing was to transcend time and would be heard through all of eternity.

Then in another place somewhere in time an apostle of our Lord heard this chicken crow and it gave him to feel true remorse in his heart. After this had happened then the spirit of the Lord was able to enter his repentant heart and help him bring forth the will of our Lord. Each man hears the chicken crow and at his own place and at his own time. This is why the chickens crowing had to come from the heart that it could transcend time and be there for each and every man when each and every man arrives at his place of hearing.

Now that the chicken has crowed and has been heard by the apostle Peter and many others we find that this story has led up to the telling of the story of the chicken that is mentioned in scripture that did serve our Lord. The egg as we all know is a function of the hen, so I have not really told that story.

However you could say, as the saying goes, that there is egg on my face for I did not see where this story was going until this part as you and I see the intent of the spirit.

Then I would point out here that I have titled this part of my book as "The Story of The Three Crows." This was it, as I do not intend to write about actual literal crows. Thus in my story the chicken came first and the egg came after.

Commentary:

If men are truly eternal as many hope is our condition, then we must be aware that eternity stretches forth in two directions, backwards and forward. Many men hope for an afterlife, hoping for a joyous eternity. Yet few men are given to contemplate eternity past.

The devil is depicted as having a tail which is a symbolic depiction indicating history. Many of us also have tails having participated in all that was before. For the most part we are unaware as to our actions in eternity past.

This creation has brought forth a savior who offers to carry the responsibility for our sins and satisfy justice for the demands of those sins. Many men fail to recognize the true importance of this opportunity for they look at the guilt of their short mortal lives failing to recognize that history may be contained in their eternal past that really wants to be washed clean. Due to the short sighted vision and that men do not currently have access to their eternal memories they fail to take action and truly cross over and take a place in the vision of light. The opportunity is ever present and the savior stands ever ready to receive all men that should arrive at a place of hearing.

Additional Commentary:

If you would have remission of your eternal sins be baptized by one holding the proper priesthood to perform that ordinance of our Lord's gospel. I believe that my story about the one chicken mentioned in scripture is more inspired than just pure imagination. I further believe that every man may in fact hear this chicken at one time in his life or in another.

I would imagine that the noise made by a snoring chicken would be similar in sound to a death rattle that is frequently heard when a person leaves this world of our mortalities. This transition from this world and life into the next I am certain will be a time of discovery in which many shall learn if they slept away great opportunity and find they have arrived at a hollow place.

Others shall arrive at this same place to behold that captured opportunity has yielded great things unto them. These shall be like unto a farmer that hearing the cock crow in the morning, as is his place, rises up and labors until sunset that in his days of harvest there may be an abundance that is ultimately greater than the man can consume alone. Thus he finds that he is able to share of his abundance and all this for he gave heed to a simple thing such as a chicken crowing.

Chapter 10
Story 5   Part 1
     I will write a story now that will start in darkness and progress into the light. This story may be strong for tender readers.

     Imagine if you would the deepest darkest jungle in Africa and in the undergrowth a cunning monster lay in wait. He is a gorilla but not just any gorilla, for this is the king of gorillas. This gorilla is a carnivore and only a carnivore.

     A little monkey nearby is playing as cute little monkeys always enjoy to play. The gorilla is waiting and watching and soon he shall have that which he desires. When the monkey finally arrives within the kill zone of the gorilla he pounces.

     Tearing limbs and flesh in a horrible carnage and flinging body parts that he knows he shall soon consume, once the rage of the kill is spent. The cute little monkey is quite dead now and torn in pieces. I have created a very dark image that will no doubt take great skill as a writer to undo and arrive at a palatable story that my reader will consider to have sufficient merit at the end to justify having received this awful image at the beginning.

So back to the story about this king of darkness the gorilla. His rage is spent his dinner lay all about him on the floor of the jungle and he is now ready to eat his prey. Reaching down to pick up and consume his first body part of the monkey he discovers a little bird upon the ground. This distracts his attention for a moment as birds are always the hardest prey to catch and quite honestly a greater delicacy because of the difficulty of obtaining them.

He is puzzled as to why this one does not fly away or try to escape for everyone in the jungle knows of this horrible gorilla. He picks up the little bird and looks closely as his mind is more curious at this moment and he has just finished a kill and is satisfied.

This is when it happened and it was not what the gorilla had expected. In fact it caught him quite surprised for as his gaze came to look into the eyes of the little bird he saw a twinkle. It was then in a brief moment that the gorilla saw and experienced his first vision of a heart. True it was a little heart and only the heart of a bird but it penetrated the gorilla to the core.

Then looking at the bird quite differently now than before he saw the little bird was injured. He realized that the bird had probably fallen victim to his recent rage and maybe had been struck by a flying object as the gorilla thrashed everything that had been in his kill zone. Holding the little bird quite gently now in his oversize hand, the big fellow comes to realize that he holds something precious in his hand. In fact he realizes he has never had anything in his hand that was more precious.

He thinks to himself I now have a problem and I must find a solution. For he knows that the nearest veterinarian is on the other side of the continent and yet this is where he must now travel. The journey is far and he knows he will encounter many obstacles on his way. So he picks up an arm and a leg from the monkey and sets off on his journey eating as he goes.

Remember that I said this was a journey from the darkness into the light and this gorilla has history that is not to be undone in a moment by a single event. Actually a single event is like a spark that can lead to a flame that can lead to a fire that can light up all of eternity given time and maintenance. The question then is who has the patience to give us maintenance that the fire can continue. The answer is God but for this story more specifically The Holy Spirit.

The gorilla walks many days and encounters a great many others on his journey and begins to look into the eyes when opportunity allows and comes to recognize other hearts. Meanwhile other gorillas begin to follow for the news that something was happening and the king was not quite right.

There had always been an ongoing struggle to hold the top position, and if this king was done for another would fill the place. This king knew his precarious position but this did not concern him for he had an important task. The other gorillas did not understand why the king did not just eat this little bird, enjoy the sweetness of the moment and move on. The king wondered himself this very thing but knew that all of creation had changed recently.

Perhaps he was the only one who knew this but it did not matter. Still he pressed on and in time he arrived to the other side and he walked into the office of the veterinarian.

Asking for medical attention for his little friend the vet asked and how will you be paying for these services today sir? Will that be cash or do you have insurance? The gorilla said are you joking or do you play with the king of the jungle? Or perhaps you do not recognize that I am that gorilla that was feared by all the darkness. The vet says I perceive sir that you may be a little off or perhaps even a lot but let us tend first to your friend for this is most pressing, then we shall address payment after. The vet then takes the bird away and tends to his injuries.

While the gorilla is alone waiting nature calls and going into the restroom he encounters a mirror. When he looks into the mirror he beholds looking back at him is the face of a man. Thus I give unto you my reader the story of evolution. The journey of man from gorilla. I admit I may have made mistakes and not been perfectly accurate for it may not have been a bird the gorilla carried it could have been a baby bunny rabbit. The point of a story such as this is to capture the essence of the matter or the heart and arrive at your destination having evolved into a thing of greater virtue than you were at the beginning.

Story 5   Part 2

This part of my gorilla story will be a blending of commentary and story. I imagine my readers are probably curious as to what happens to our gorilla-man after he leaves the office of the veterinarian and I will try to present some possibilities.

He goes back into the jungle from whence he had come but he knew he was now different. The act of caring outside of himself had begun a transformation that would run its course in due time. The Holy Spirit was also determined this should be for this gorilla was chosen to actually be the king. Now before his transformation the gorilla had falsely perceived himself as a king but this had been an illusion, for a king must be capable of thinking beyond himself and just because this gorilla had been the most ferocious beast in the jungle did not make him a king.

He knew that should he not accept what was upon him it would create a void and that a void always seeks to fill itself that it not remain a void, this is a simple rule of creation. The gorilla-man knew that the other gorillas were lacking what it took to be king, they had the ability to be ferocious but it would take more than this to be a king.

Another could in time learn but how long would that take and would an incident such as what this fellow had experienced happen to another or would it take a long time for another to experience such an event as the one that had transformed this one gorilla into a man.

The gorilla-man decided he would keep his position. For he could see no way to step down and not have responsibility for all the evil that could and probably would follow in the jungle. If he should choose to let the position pass or if he should create a void by going into the world of men. He had a desire to do just that but he was now between the rock and the hard place, for having experienced the feelings of a man his heart was no longer just of the jungle.

As the gorilla-man walked through the jungle in contemplation of his condition he encountered other gorillas and he noticed that they acted strange in his presence. It was almost as if their fear and respect had greatly increased. It in fact had for they now looked upon him as being unpredictable and this can be a scary element in a being of true power.

The gorilla-man thought to himself that this was not a negative but could in fact help him as he now had concern for all of the other creatures in the jungle. He knew that senseless killing would no longer be tolerated. He knew that everyone still had to eat but this killing for the lust of rage would be put to an end and he was just the gorilla man that could enforce just such a concept.

In time he came to notice that as he walked through his jungle and encountered gorillas or men they each saw a different face. For men saw him clearly as another man and gorillas saw him as the king and yet a gorilla. He was just extremely scary to them for he had blended worlds and crossed some lines.

One day as he walked through his jungle he came upon a beehive and he thought about this. And he thought you know the bees are a hard working lot that tend to their own affairs. Yet the bear is inclined to rob them of all their efforts and feed himself with total disregard of others. So I think another story is in order as we consider just what is the bears problem that he would persist in doing such a thing, and repetitively.

Then in closing this segment about the gorilla-man for now at least I see that he is alone and has become one of a kind. This is not a good thing, for we all need others of our species to give us joy one in each other. I now see that in another story perhaps I will need to write about other gorillas crossing over and becoming men of compassion. Having the problems of others in their new hearts and losing their ferocity as they set about the task of keeping order within the jungle.

Not for the sake of self and the struggle for position but rather that they will be there to assist those in need. Thus I am given to consider that if this should happen and an entire race of gorilla-men should come forth they will need a name to describe this new species. So I will name the group now and I choose that they shall be called G-Men.

So in another time or another story I will need to write more about the virtues of my G-Men. For remember like the prickly pear all are needing a worthy story and my newly created race of G-Men are no exception. Someone ultimately needs to write well of them. I just never imagined I would be the one to contemplate such a thing. But then this is a story about crossing lines.

And also about gaining understanding of the stories of others. This is after all what gives us compassion, is having the greater understanding of the conditions and perspectives of a vast many other ways of thinking.

Chapter 11

Story 6

The day had almost arrived and the family was all getting very excited for the event had been waited on with great anticipation. Junior could not stop talking about it and had driven everyone else in the family more than a little tired of hearing about it. Yet they all understood his excitement and understanding always gives compassion.

Mom, Pop and Sis were now almost as excited as junior had been for the longest time. The extended family was also buzzing about the upcoming event. They had all been watching the calendar also in great anticipation. Then it came and everyone gathered to send mom, pop, sis and junior on their way.it was a joyous occasion for great anticipation of an event always makes the event sweeter and even a little bigger than life. So it was with this event and had always been, even as far back as the old ones could remember.

When the flight began the birds were singing and the sun was shining and the sky was as blue as it had ever been. It was a good day and as the four went on their way they had a song in their hearts and perhaps on their lips. One cannot be certain for it was always hard to hear over the buzz, but let's assume the song found its way to their lips. Our four thus went singing as they went.

Over trees they went, over streams they went, even over a big old mountain. Then they saw it and it was truly beauty to behold. You may ask at this point just what they found and it is my intention to reveal exactly that to you my reader. I will tell you now it was the best clover pasture in this whole part of the country, and it was in full bloom.

Well you may ask just what was so special about a blooming pasture of clover. I would say not much unless you are a cow or a bee. Well my story, this story is about a family of bees, mom, pop, sis, and the extended family we will call the hive. The event, this event was the first day of spring.

The hive always selected one family to be the family that would go first into the pasture and commence to collect this year's collection of pollen. With which to produce next year's crop of honey that would sustain the hive until the next year's batch, and so on, as it had always been and would ever be so. This was a source of great joy to be selected as the family and it was given by selection by the queen herself. How could those chosen by the queen not have joy in the event?

Thus the family spent this first day of spring in joy, about the business given them by the queen. Knowing they would return with great information to share with all the hive about the condition of the pasture for this specific year. Like what areas were thickest in blossom and the condition of the pollen, how many other hives had sent forth families and what territories each family had chosen for their hives.

Then as is always the case the day started to come to an end and the event was nearing completion. It had been a perfect day and with glad hearts the family mom, pop, sis and junior began the journey home.

It was then a bad feeling came to them and they perceived something was not right. This feeling intensified as they got closer and closer to their home. Then they saw the most horrid sight that a bee could ever realize in his life for the home was destroyed and the family shattered.

The villain yet present stood there boldly and brazenly, with pieces of the broken hive still in his sticky fingers as he continued to gorge himself on the honey that had been brought forth by the hard and honest work of the hive.

He was not concerned about the trauma this would cause in the lives of the little ones and in fact he cared about no one else or any of the consequences of his actions. The only thing he cared about was satisfying his insatiable appetite for the sweetness he had once experienced a long time ago. This bear had history and he had destroyed many others on his journey of self as he walked with complete disregard for others.

The End

Commentary:

I expect my reader is saying wait just a minute, I expect a happy ending to a story that I take the time to read. The reality is that this story does not have a happy ending. In order to arrive at a happy end one must have feelings beyond just yourself and empathy for the effect our actions may bring into the lives of others. When all men begin to understand this principal then we shall see about putting a new ending on this story.

I have written many stories about many imaginary and fictitious characters. You my reader may identify with some completely and parts of others and even a blending of a great many.

The only true villain I have brought forth is the bear. This is the character I would warn you not to find in your image. If this is who you truly are then we are helpless and you are hopeless for this image is without solution.

If you are an emulation of the bear you might be best advised to do some changing. For the time of cleaning house has arrived. The day of tolerance has passed, at least tolerance for this image of the bear. We shall yet have tolerance of those that would truly clean house, but a bear pretending shall convince no one. For

we shall see through to his heart and judge
if his intent is to harm others with
disregard. Thus we arrive at a time of
definition, good and evil, self and selfless.

Story 7

A long, long, time ago I lay alone in the darkness. I knew that I was alone for nothing yet existed, there was only me. I was in the darkness for the light did not yet exist. I thus lay in the darkness and I did not move for I knew that if I moved good and evil would emanate from the action of my motion. I greatly desired the good but I knew that condemnation for the evil would capture my soul and require accountability. So there I lay for as long a time as one can imagine, afraid to move but yet being fully aware and in great torment as I contemplated possible consequences to myself should I ever choose to move.

Finally the torment was too great and I determined that the consequence I would embrace and so I stretched forth my hand. When I thus reached outward I touched someone. It does not matter the gender be it a he or a she, but now I was no longer alone. When I lay in the darkness afraid to move I was truly alone but having overcome my fear the first realized consequence is that another presence was with me. Had I not moved I would yet be alone.

My second movement was to speak and thus I asked who is there? The presence responded I am your father and thus a great portion of my fears were overcome for a man shall gain confidence in the presence of his father. Had the presence answered I am the boogey-man then I would be writing a much different story than the version I now write.

Thus a long, long, time ago I lay in the darkness with the presence of my father and we were alone. I conversed with my father and told him I was alone but when I found the courage to take action and stretch forth my hand he came to have presence with me. I learn from my experience that the good is greatly desirable yet I know that evil is present, even if it is not yet revealed.

My father told me I am aware of your dilemma and I also understand that every action brings forth both good and evil but behold what happens when I stretch forth my hand. I looked as my father did thus and I saw nothing for we were yet in darkness but when my father had stretched forth his hand I sensed a much greater presence was with us.

My father then asked who is there and the voices of a vast and even, perhaps an infinite number answered back we are the family of our father. Yet we all lay in darkness, but the darkness was not as bad as it had been when I had been completely alone. Then our father spoke again and he said we are a family now and we have embraced the darkness, let the power of balance have its effect that we reside in the light. When he had thus spoken the light came upon us and we could behold with sight the wonderful family of our father.

Then we all had joy having departed from the darkness and our joy was in the presence of our companions in the family of our father. Then our father declared to us a simple truth as he told us you exist that you might have this joy one in each other and nothing else is truth except this.

Then he declared the darkness will try to take this from you at some point in time and it will use the concept of self to steal you away from the presence of your family. This is the evil that balance brings forth for even the father stretching forth his mighty hand could not escape that both good and evil emanate from the action of motion.

I look about me now in the world and I see the concept of self is what would take us, and as many as it can, into the darkness to be alone as the self seeks to overcome the action of our father when he assembled his family. The consequence of the action of motion is already upon us, if we should reach out to others now, we run the risk of looking foolish perhaps. We do not need to convert all others to our way of thinking.

We only need to locate the one other person in whose heart we shall become perfect and make certain that he or she is also tied to someone else and thus holding hands in a symbolic sort of way we all arrive together in our new place. We may pass through more darkness yet, but as long as our father does not abandon us, his family we shall be alright.

Remember it was he that gave us light originally and joy also. We can regain these two elements in unison with others but not alone. Then finally I would call attention to the age old saying that the road to hell is paved with good intentions. And I would say that if that is the case then pave a good road for our father will not leave us forever in hell. And when we shall find that we have been released, should it be our fate to experience hell, then we shall need a good road to take us back quickly to the presence of our family. That we might make up for all of our lost time as we fully explored the concept and consequence of the self.

Commentary:

In this story I explore the concept of being alone and existing before all things to illustrate a concept. What I have written in between the lines is that as a person explores the concept of self that person can in fact exist alone until he stretches forth his hand. Or in other words until he reaches out to others and his awareness begins to become conscious of others occupying the same place as he and that these others ultimately should be considered as his family.

With that said I would bring to the awareness of my reader that the theories of evolution and of creation both arrive at the same final conclusion and that is that we are all family. They both arrive at this conclusion through a very different process but they both arrive at the correct conclusion, so I am satisfied in both.

If I had two children and I said to them both bring me a math equation that arrives at a correct solution of four as an answer. Then one child came with an equation of 1+3, and the other came with an equation of 2+2, I as a parent would have joy in both of my children for having solved the problem that I gave them to ponder.

Then I also equate this feeling of self as evil and it is in its place. If a person can rediscover what is important then they will have opportunity to find lost and missing companions. This then can become a source of the greater joy having lost all to find it again.

Conclusion For Part 2, 2003

We have all seen an individual of questionable sanity standing in the street proclaiming that the end is coming or even that it is upon us. We for the most part give little attention assuming that the individual so proclaiming is either a little or a lot insane. This is probably an accurate assessment, however at some point in time their proclamation shall have validity and contain great truth.

We should all be thankful that the voices those individuals hear in their minds do not have presence in our minds, for any man could find himself called to service. Is there scripture or written word anywhere in which the Lord declares he will only use intelligent and perfectly sane individuals to vocalize a warning unto the inhabitants of mortality?

Usually these individuals are ones that have been overcome and destroyed by the structure of society we have created. When the world falls upon you will your mind be strong enough to resist chaos? Are not all men susceptible to all things equally and but for the grace of God there goes I.

what warning would you sound in the hour of your madness?

I have passed through a time of struggling and looked deeply into the darkness and come to learn a few profound truths. I would write about inner and outer darkness for I believe that one the Lord can abide and one he cannot. The separation is the heart felt desire to hurt others, this is the darkness the Lord cannot abide.

This is what will drag a man into hell and if hell is not sufficient to bring forth a change of heart will then quite possibly drag the man out of this creation entirely and leave the man in literal outer darkness. Can a man so afflicted ever find his way back into the creation?

Assuming such a place as outer darkness exist and it may not. For another alternative possibility is that the man filled with great hatred is taken back into the light perhaps into heaven itself and there left to feel the love even perfect love of all those that have overcome the madness of hatred. This man could find his condition more torturous than that of a man on the outside.

I ultimately do not know all these things and thus I write about things that I do know about. I write about tolerance of others except those that would hurt others with lack of feeling and devoid of empathy. I write about finding your virtues and coming forth from darkness. I write about truth in fiction format.

There are a great many given authority to reveal truth and I am not one of these learned and inspired men. I am but a man telling stories and somewhere in this world is a friend, the one friend, the one that shall give me joy. For there is a promise that if a man should labor all the days of his life and bring but one friend with him into the kingdom of our Lord how great shall be their joy.

I went to the edge of chaos to gain understanding of a very simple principal, but then I have always been prone to do things the hard way. I know that you are undoubtedly much wiser than I was, thus your way should be much easier, this is a good thing. I hope that at the very least my stories may have distracted you from your own harshness of life or given you even the tiniest moments of enjoyment. For if they accomplish at least this then they shall have accomplished what I created them for. I would awaken the wisdom that is in you my reader for the door of light is also within the hearts of all men for balance requires this be so.

You cannot have a north but you also have a south. You cannot have inner darkness but that you also have the potential for inner light. They are however dissimilar and only one can have dominance and guide the actions of a man. The self and the selfless is in fact the same as the dark and the light or the good and the evil. He that has greatest sense of self will have the greatest struggle to find the light within his own heart. Good luck to each and all as you wrestle with your demons.

Conclusion 2017:

All that I wrote in 2003 was by inspiration. So I have presented that here with very little changes and modifications. Since that time I have gained a greater understanding of all things. So I present to you additional conclusions in 2017. One item I would call your attention to is my method of titling my work. When I was quite young there was a show called Aesop's Fables. This show would present two titles for an episode with the word "or" separating the two titles. This is my inspiration in my titles.

Part 1 of my work I wrote in 2017, part 2, I wrote in 2003, I decided this was acceptable because the scriptures declare that the last shall be first and the first shall be last. I know this is not what the scripture refers to but I decided that it is appropriate for my work as well.

God the Father has given unto me a family of all those who become perfect. This was done to give me balance and support for eternity forward. This family is in addition to the family of my mortality. I would point out that perfection exist on

two extremes one is when we are found to be lacking nothing the other is when we are found to be lacking everything. On one extreme we find
the Sons of God on the other extreme we find the Sons of Perdition.

These two will join efforts in bringing forth life. The war between the two will soon come to an end. But not before their respective tests, that will precede the corruption of their perfection. This does not mean we cannot remain close to being perfect but it shall provide relief and make it possible for God to maintain balance in his creation that it might continue to unfold.

Perdition so far as I am aware has three meanings. The first is it refers to a place where we suffer for darkness, of which are greatest tormentor is our own conscience. The second is it refers to Cain and the third is it refers to Lucifer. I call these two perdition senior and perdition junior.

My own torment of conscience has been undone by the test which came upon me and whatever happens next or wherever I end up I will be okay. My eternal desire has been to gain a family as my fathers have. I have accomplished that and if you find yourself to be a member of my family I say behold thou art my brother and welcome.

Then we come to the mission which Jesus chose me to serve him on in my mortality and this is something I must accomplish for he truly chose my son to replace me should I decline or fail to fulfill his will. This is something I cannot allow to pass to another. So I persist in trying to accomplish this task set before me. But the end is not entirely in my hand alone so I ask you give unto me your assistance.

If you are the Apostle chosen to eat up a little book such as this one, or perhaps in fact this one, I say unto you that thou art the king that was known as Uriel. Further your priesthood authority in the other world is third and thus you outrank me. So should we serve a mission unto the house of Israel in the last days I shall be your junior companion.

Unto he that stands one foot upon the earth and one foot upon the sea, and upon whose head is a bow, or the covenant of God, in whose hand I am but an open book, I say I have received your vision of darkness unto its end, and my test did come and I did receive a family by the hand of God. I would ask of thee give unto me a fathers blessing that will seal upon us both our history as well as our future.

Now I will give a message to those that ever were or ever shall be given life or the ability to act, find your virtue and give unto it perfect expression, meaning that it is lacking nothing, and this promise I give you, you will for a time become one with God. Corruption will ultimately bring you down from this high but not before you gain great understanding. Many say I will become perfect in the future, but I say unto them you are missing great opportunity for this is something we can accomplish now in the present.

Then finally I would bear my testimony that Jesus is the Christ and the Church of Jesus Christ of Latter Day Saints is his church offering to all men and women the saving ordinances of his gospel. And then one more item I would call attention